I0133291

TOMORROW'S ROSE

Poems and Thoughts

LARE JOSEPH AUSTIN

Tomorrow's Rose: A collection of poetry and a few thoughts

Cedar Street Books

Copyright © 2017 by Lare Joseph Austin

lareandk7@gmail.com

First edition, published 2017

All rights reserved

This book is protected under the copyright laws of the United States of America. In accordance with the U.S. Copyright Act of 1976, no part of this publication may be reproduced, stored in a retrieval system, or transmitted, in any form or by any means without the prior written permission of the author. Any reproduction or other unauthorized use of the material or artwork herein is prohibited.

Credits: Cover & Illustrations by Karen B. Austin

Table of Contents

PUPPIES N KITTENS   1

CRAYONS   2

HANDFULS OF RICE   4

SONGS OF THE CRICKET   6

CONCERTO   8

THE SMELL OF FALL   10

OLD JUANITO   12

MAGNOLIA   14

LEARNING   16

THE PARROT WANTS TO TALK   18

PEBBLES   21

GRANDFATHER CLOCK   22

MY BACKYARD   24

MOMENTARY STORM   26

EURHYTHMICS   28

SUNSET ON THE SAWTELLE   29

FROM THE WATER'S EDGE   32

CABERNET SAUVIGNON   33

WATER PUDDLES   36

CANDLE   38

THERE ARE TIMES   40

JUST BEFORE SUNRISE   42

GUARDIAN ANGEL   43

VETERANS DAY   44

WAITING FOR NOVEMBER   46

ME AND SALLY   47

THE BOARD   50

CATCH   52

UBIQUITY   54

HER EYES TOLD ME   56

I MUST BE GETTING OLD   57

WHAT I SEE   58

THE ROCK   60

PENCILS   62

SWEATLODGE   63

FLOYD   64

FROM YOUR BALCONY   66

THE MONARCH AND THE CROW   68

SPARROW   70

MOTHER'S DAY   72

DADS AND RADISHES   74

HAPPINESS IS MY WARM BATHROBE   76

FARMER'S MARKET   78

SO BEE IT   80

PRINCIPLES   82

MESTIZO   85

JOURNEY   88

ONE OF THOSE DAYS   90

NEEDLE   91

SONG   92

THE NIGHT   93

TOMATO   94

BISCUITS   96

HONOR GUARD   98

SPANISH RICE   100

LIFE BEGINS AT FIFTY   102

MOCKINGBIRD   104

SNAIL   106

THE TWO OLD MEN   108

SLAPPING TORTILLAS   110

I KNOCKED ONLY ONCE   112

GRAPEFRUIT   114

TEACHING   115

TULE FOG   116

DAYLIGHT SAVINGS TIME   118

WINTER'S CALLING   119

SOUTH DAKOTA   120

THE PERFECT DAY   123

CONTINENTAL BREAKFAST   124

THOUGHTS OF DAD   128

THREE DAYS IN THE SUN   130

IF I COULD ONLY ASK   132
WHEN THE WIND AND
        THE GRASS COME TO THE CEDARS   134

THE WILLOW   137

THE OAK AND THE OWL   138

THE BOOKSTORE   140

WORM   142

YOSEMITE   144

THE FOX AND THE SQUIRREL   146

WAY OF THE DREAMCATCHER   148

SERENITY   149

THE FROG THAT HELD THE STARS   150

TOMORROW'S ROSE   152

A FEW SHORT THOUGHTS   153

*For all those
fighting the good fight
against breast cancer*

All proceeds from this book
will be donated to breast cancer research

Puppies N Kittens

What is it about puppies n kittens that
makes your face smile and your heart melt and
allowed you not a single feeling of guilt when
you were at the shelter and
picked up the puppy and said
"I'll take this one," and
then picked up the kitten and said
"I'll take this one, as well."

Puppies n kittens…at least these two…
are focused on only one thing at a time
and for now that one thing is playing and
rolling together on the carpet like a
single ball of yarn covered in two shades of fur.

Tonight they will slumber soundly
at the foot of my bed.
In the morning the kitten will have my
pillow all to herself (don't ask me how
this happens) and when the puppy tries to
snuggle next to her
the kitten, with her tiny, soft paw of fluffy pads
will gently swat him on his chin and puppy will
curl back down
below her pillow.

Back to sleep.

CRAYONS

The old man and the little boy
sat together before breakfast
drawing, scribbling on
wrinkled sheets of paper. The aroma

of eggs poaching and
muffins toasting
sifted throughout their
kitchen playground as
the two of them sipped their glasses of
orange juice. The small

boy proudly turned his
scattered lines toward the old man.
Realizing that he didn't understand what
the lines meant, the boy pointed
to the old man's white, handlebar mustache.
The man touched his forefinger to his
furry upper lip then nodded with a smile.
The boy triumphantly clapped his hands and
rewarded himself with another
sip of his juice. Not yet

able to read and write
the boy would not understand
even if the Alzheimer's disease
would permit the old man to scribble the words
he so wished to express to the boy. In his

forever silent world the boy understood.

He took his crayon and
scratched out on his own, smaller
wrinkled piece of paper the very first
thing he had ever been taught in his
infant world of sign language.
A serrated picture of a single hand showing
the universal symbol for

'I love you'.

The child wiped the tear from
his grandfather's eye
then took another sip of his orange juice.

HANDFULS OF RICE

What is it that geese chat about
in the morning when flying
low and swift to
wherever they are going? Are they

honking to encourage those leading
their choreographed formation to
keep up their speed? Is it

the hungry, young goslings asking
why the flock is not stopping
at the tender alfalfa?
And if not at the alfalfa why not
at the field of corn.
And if not at the corn,
if not there, then…
where are they going? The cows

are already bunched in their
favorite small corner at the
water basin watching their calves
drinking and have no interest in the geese
landing next to them,
flaring their broad wings and
stretched webbed feet. Under an

early morning sky of solid pewter
the geese have come again for
the handfuls of rice I have
laid out for them, their honking
now replaced with the sounds of
joyful foraging, especially
from the goslings.

I am envious.

I wish I knew how to speak Geese.

For another handful of rice
will they teach me?

Songs of the Cricket

I do not have to put my cupped hand
to my ear to hear them.
They will come.
I do not have to hold my breath
waiting to detect them.
They will find me
as they always do. They begin

very faintly, awakening
delicate taps within my ears
that others may possibly
not even be aware of,
or, accept them as
part of the hollow ambiance
that comes with an early,
warm moist night. But I

hear them, I know them.
Tonight I am serenaded by
songs of the cricket.
Oh how they lightly
surround me,
enfold me. Little cricket,

the nighttime is your world
but where are you hidden?
You dance your nocturnal songs
for me to hear, but you are
not for me to see. You carry

me through yet another night
and I, in turn, must let you go. And so

my gentle friend, in this
my moment of solitude
you let my mind once again
bathe in calm thoughts and gentle feelings.
And my heart is once again
magically filled with
songs of the cricket.

CONCERTO

Johann Sebastian Bach
played on cd while gentle
flames from hot burning oak
danced in our fireplace
to the tempo of
"Concerto for Violin and Strings
in A-minor" all the while

blending…folding with the persistent
chiming of the pouring 10 p.m.
rain outside, cascading down
closed shuttered windows…it was…

poetry…I promise…magical verse
spontaneously being discovered in
real time…everything rendering
in real time…breathing the
stanzas from the precision of the
orchestra…glowing to the
smell of soft, wafting smoke from the fire…
emotions crescendoing in our
most private harmony, our magical
sequence, we held to our very own
timeline…rejoicing, prancing on

celebrations of
quarter notes and octaves from
the lowest chords to the
highest pitches of compositions:
heat and passion climaxing in
explosions of vibrato and reverberation
that came from

"Concerto for Violin and Strings in
A-minor" by
Johann Sebastian Bach

THE SMELL OF FALL

I love summer.
Don't we all?
Playing in long days until
the hot sun melts into
amber warm nights filled with
hidden crickets and frogs
singing beneath
full moons and bright stars
ushering in cool mornings
that greet my wicker basket filled
with sweet apricots, and
when these barefoot days
fade with the last
of the summer fruit

I will miss them
but I will still rise early

for now nature begins
twirling her paintbrush
and the world becomes
her canvas filled with
brilliant bright skies shining
upon the aspens with their
golden leaves
dancing in
placid breezes

to the delight of the ears and,
oh my, the aromas of the dry grass
and the ripened, tart crab apples
after being moistened by thin

morning fog, and when

I walk under the young walnuts
hiding in their thin, dark brown husks
I will thank the sage and thyme
for their delicious fragrances as well.

Come walk with me...
don't forget your sweater.

I love the smell of fall.
Don't we all?

OLD JUANITO

On the north shore of Lake Chapala
sits the small, quiet Mexican town of San Juan.
There was not much there.
But there was old Juanito.

No-one really knew for sure his real name.
No matter how many times you asked,
he would simply smile and extend his weathered,
sun scarred hand to your chest and say,
"Usted puede llamar a mí Juanito." (You may call me Juanito.)
as if you were meeting him for the first time.

Every mid-morning he would
lead his slow burro that pulled his faded,
canvased cart down a particular,
narrow cobble stone street on his way to the
small dirt park on the water's edge.
The kids on that street knew
the clip-pity clop of that burro and
by ones and twos
would draw to his cart that paraded
the hand written words 'Paletas Juanito'
to exchange their centavos
for his hand made lollypops.

By the time he reached the park he would
have none left for the old men
sitting quietly with their gray faced dogs
that yawned a lot.
Seeing Juanito, the old men would

smile and join him at the single,
crusted table there
because for them Juanito brought
something more desirable than
paletas.

Juanito would reach through the
small opening in the canvas that
covered his cart where he brought out
the paletas for the kids but now brought out
a newly corked, homemade bottle
of mescal that he served to the old men
in clean, paper-coned cups.
Juanito always insisted serving his mescal
in clean paper-coned cups and
before anyone drank he always led with
"La gracia y el equilibrio en todas las cosas."
(Grace and poise in all things.)
Salud.

MAGNOLIA

If you have a magnolia tree to go to…
go to it.

You do not have to sit under it.
You do not have to stand beneath it.
You do not have to count all of its
showy springtime blossoms and
glossy leaves.
You do not have to thank it for its
sweet fragrance or even say hello
to the leaping songbirds that have
come for its fruit.

You simply just need to
go to it…it will do the rest. My magnolia

is where I go for usually no particular
reason or want or intention and it is
perfectly fine with me curling quietly
on top of its roots to write my notes
about…anything, because it is
always busy with its pollinating and
providing its protection and its
fleshy aril to the birds that visit it. The other

afternoon I fell asleep under my tree.
I dreamed that a small songbird was
mischievously tickling my nose and
would not stop until I woke. And when

I did wake I was not at all surprised to
find no such bird on top of me, or even
near me except those fluttering
in the high branches above me.
The late day coolness was now here, hinting
to me it was time to go home and as I sat up
my notepad and pencil slid off my chest and
a tiny, fluffy feather

fell
    from
        my
            face.

LEARNING

When did you first realize it?
Did it come to you subtly?
Like late summer thick fog that
in early evening slowly crawls in
from the sleeping surf, silently over the beach,
to sprinkle your tongue and
dance with your fire pit? Was it

the time when you watched the doe mule deer
silently command her fawn to
snap from its graze of berries
back to her mother's side
and dutifully follow her
through the high grass meadow to
the safety of their thicket
near the water. Or, was it

when you saw the disobedient baby blackbird
try to fly from its nest before it was time
only to tumble all the way down
to the broad, muddied roots of the tree
and be instantly snatched up by
a patiently waiting hungry bobcat.

Perhaps you heard it. Or perhaps when

you became conscious
through blank eyes biting
the frost from the air.
Not everyone or everything
learns the same way.
Some learn through listening.
Some through seeing.
Some through doing.

And then

some never

learn at all.

THE PARROT WANTS TO TALK

Her white whiskers stayed perfectly still
beneath her black tipped nose
her tail slowly swaying
like an upturned pendulum
back and forth
back and forth
in perfect unison with her
fixed brown eyes
watching…
watching.

The young calico
had never seen a hummingbird
buzzing so close to her
pine fence perch.

The hummingbird
was darting in and out of
newly awakened red flowers
gathering presents of sweet nectar
when it noticed the kitten's
curious surveillance.

"If I bring some nectar
will you let me share it with you?"
the hummingbird asked.

"Yes," said the calico, her whiskers
twitching joyously at
the thought of a new friend.
"I would like that very much."

The hummingbird quickly returned
with some nectar, but instead of
sharing, it gobbled up the nectar
in front of the kitten's nose.

"If I bring a juicy bug
will you let me share it with you?"
the hummingbird asked.

Who can refuse a juicy bug?

"Yummy," said the calico.
The hummingbird promptly
returned again, but
instead of sharing the bug
it gobbled it up
right in front of the kitten.
The young feline realized
the hummingbird was teasing her.

"Why do you tease me like this?"
asked the calico.

"Because I can," said the hummingbird,
then flew off before the kitten could
swat at it with her pillowy paw.

Well…the parrot had been observing
this from just outside his cage and
knew something the young calico
did not.

He knew where the hummingbird
sleeps at night.

The kitchen window is open.

The parrot wants to talk.

PEBBLES

We lobbed pebbles
into a delicate pond early this evening.
Just my wife and I.
Quiet thoughts.
Alone. We waited until the only kid with his
fishing line had left. The air

was moist, and warm.
Still.
Fishing spiders swiftly glided
across the water's glass surface
looking to hide for the night while
the staleness from the
thick patches of
dark green moss folded
into our nostrils. I quietly

uttered a small word.
Maybe, half a word. I barely heard
myself say it. Don't know what I said.
Gibberish? My wife

flicked a small twig onto
the top of a small, narrow floating
moss patch. Our island.
And softly said, "I know…me too…"

We lobbed our fragile pebbles
just the two of us
hand in hand
into our pond this evening.

GRANDFATHER CLOCK

It stands patiently, vigilant
at its station next to the
double glass doors, partially hidden by
long, slender laced sheers where
its music chimes down the outside
step-railing from the porch
to the honeysuckle growing
at the wooden gate and though

the honeysuckle will never
grow high enough to see this
longcase timepiece, with its
fading oak cabinet garlanded with
carvings of flowers and wheat stalks,
it adores the clock's seductive
Westminster melody producing a

most harmonious marriage between
the sweetness of the young
honeysuckle and the tranquil
songs from the old grandfather clock,
their vows renewing themselves
every quarter hour, each sway

of the pendulum in perfect balance
with the timing of precisely crafted
bushings and gears and
hammers and rods working
so silently the only thing heard is the
slow, steady drip from the
rain gutter until the next chime, prompting

memories of mere, less hectic
times of colorful greeting cards
at 4 o'clock tea and
lessons from elders to be
patient and wise with your life and
the morals that you take to, and if

you simply listen you will know why
everyone loves a grandfather clock, especially
when it chimes at the top of the hour
telling you it is time
to take the oatmeal cookies from the oven.

MY BACKYARD

I do not consider myself lucky that I have
an ocean for a backyard.
There are those who do not believe it
lucky at all to be in the solitude of their pine forests or
in the fertileness of their valleys growing vegetables and
digging worms from dark rich dirt to fish rivers.
They are where they are.
They are fulfilled and they have
no need to tell you. And so

it is for me with my ocean, and if you do not
have an ocean I will share mine with you.
Start where you are. Close your eyes.
Listen…

listen to the ocean faintly calling
with its clear voice anointing
hazy, tepid sun bristling with
fibers of a nippy breeze dancing on
your bare arms while wet sand
bristles between your toes and
salt mist flushes your eyeballs and
the sound of the surf
rinses your mind, allowing

your heart to fill with deep ocean minerals
that splinter and disintegrate all the
bad tastes from the big city, the hurtful
mass ideas and the ways of living that
kill simple joys. Behind you,

above the soft, hot blanket of beach
the palms sway their green branch fingers
in recurring ebb and flow
like the hand of a chalk pastel artist
lightly stroking a canvas of
dark blue sky. You need

not do anything more. The water will
guide your rejuvenated feet to where
the tiny sand crabs burrow.

An ocean. In your own backyard.
Isn't it wonderful.

MOMENTARY STORM

What is it about a mid-summer storm that
seems to mesmerize us? Is it because it
captures our admiration?
Does its power make us envious? Or jealous?
Do we long for some moment of
solitary company with the rainclouds? I know

when they are coming.
I smell them. I can feel them.
I do not have to see the black clouds,
swollen with their unsoiled water,
to know when they are here. They stream

and drift in before the night has
had its chance to conceal them,
ringing my inner voice to shout
"Hurry boy,
they are waiting there for you." I run

from the porch and
trust my bare feet to quickly
get me to the grassy knoll
just beyond the creek,
the first droplets
glancing off my face. At the knoll

I am ready and the thunderheads,
with me as their witness,
wait no longer to
shatter the heavens with
dashes of lightening and
piercing thunder. And rain.
So much rain. In short time

the skies grow silent. Still.
It is over.
The storm has emptied itself
and the earth is once again
purified before the morning,
when the robin will be singing
to the snails but
the snails will not be listening to her
for they will be too busy
looking for drier ground.

EURHYTHMICS

There is nothing like
the smell of cool, moist
chlorifilled air radiating from
early morning grass
in late spring when the

first golden rays of the sun
sweetly score glistening
water droplets still clinging to
petal tips of awakening
purple asters, each flower

in its decision to revel and ride
in eurhythmic dance to
a most gentle air brush that is
but a faint whisper, as if

interpreting improvised
musical compositions in
freestyle involvement, these
delicate blossoms delight in their
fragile understanding of
mother nature at her
daybreak best and therefore it is

these motions, these teachings,
that are reminders about
our own ride through life
confirming to us
it does not matter
where our ride is going or
where it might eventually take us,
what matters is
deciding to get on.

Sunset on the Sawtelle

The stellar-jays were laughing.
They were convinced
I was lost. In the

crisp, thin air of the
Northern California Sierras
their incessant
scoffing…mocking
penetrate through tall pines
like piercing arrowheads.
I almost could not blame them. I was

tired…thirsty…carefully descending a
steep, narrow tributary just off
the wider, upper Yuba Loop Trail
watching the sun being pulled
down to the ridge top.
Cool shadows were beginning
to emerge, reclaiming their
late afternoon turf. Beneath me

perhaps a quarter mile, or so
I could hear the sound of
snow runoff from the
Yuba river, its power and
churning weaving with
the swishing winds that
were swaying the tips
of the pointed trees. I had

hiked the upper Yuba loop
once before and had grown
just enough embryonic arrogance
to believe I had acquired
the ability to conquer just about
any trail that lay before me,

which naturally included
any shortcut off the main trail that
might get me back down
to the trailhead. The thought
"What the hell am I doing?"
never occurred to me.
I assumed this small offshoot I was
clumsily slithering down
migrated to the river as well.
At least,
I thought this should. This morning

began from the river,
at the upper Yuba trailhead.
The start of a steady incline
framed with the fragrance of
sweet briars and thick evergreens
that eventually crests and loops
at the top of the ridge. The stellar-jays

were there, following me…talking.
They talked all day.
They talked amongst themselves.
And I'm sure about me.
And until now
the conversation was kept polite. But now

I was on this hidden,
virtually vertical
crusted corridor that was
little more than a
dried up water capillary that
I hoped would soon dissolve back to
the river and at, or at least near,
the main trailhead. I became

conscious of my head
bobbing like a yo-yo
between monitoring my
sliding feet and the spectacular views of

the high ridge above me
and the cool, shaded canyon below
where the river rushed. When I

finally breached the base
of my trail the sight and sound of
the river was almost overwhelming.
The stellar-jays had abandoned me but
in their place was a most
spectacular sight of
the last of the warm, golden sun
dipping behind the tall ridge.
Shooting streaks
of amber and gold light were
dancing with the breezes
through the lush, green needles of
the magnificent pines. Before me

at the foot of the trail,
camouflaged in thick overgrowth of
rocks and coarse sand was a
decaying, splintered, short
wooden post with the
barely visible, readable word
'Sawtelle' carved on it. Although I

would hike the upper Yuba loop
several more times since then
I never found that particular
tiny splinter of a trail again.
But I shall never forget
that one, exhilarating time
I experienced that most glorious
sunset on the Sawtelle.

FROM THE WATER'S EDGE

When you go to your fishpond
you do not go there to discover
such things as revelations or
answers to elusive, age old questions

no, nothing like that at all
you go there because your inner being
needs to be there

you know this because
your sandals are already off your feet
letting the last steps over cool dirt and clover
prepare you for the water that is
whispering to you to
breathe and listen
listen to your earth
listen to your water
allow earth's nectar to
soothe you… heal you…and

then you must play…and

let your toes giggle with
the mud and pollywogs.

A wonderfully melting thought is
hiding just around the corner from
your heart but right now you are still
searching your soul for the answer.

CABERNET SAUVIGNON

He had simply fallen in love with her.
His first moments of
fragmented bursts of
infatuation had resolutely
melded into true love.
For the rest of his life he knew. She was

the one for him. And now he
wished to demonstrate his love…his
devotion to her by toasting a
glass of wine to her.

There is, he thought, just something
nice, or, something even special
when sipping a glass of wine.

He pondered: was it

perhaps just the feel of
the glass in one's hand?
Or, the color of the wine
as it appears through
the texture and color
of the glass? The light

from the small, square window
just behind her face gently
sparkled through his
small, liquid filled
cathedral with such
iridescent transparency. For this

particular moment he believed
red wine married well with

this simple glass.
A glass, he believed, solely meant
to hold only a red wine. And, not
too dark of a red wine, mind you.
Through the glass
the light must be allowed to
naturally transform into
softer brilliance, presenting itself in
perfect temperature. Almost…intoxicating,
his visual senses were enfolding him
with clasping contentment.
Yes, he thought,
the glass he was holding must be
as perfect as the wine that was in it.

She sat so still…so quiet.
He adored the smoothness in her cheeks.
He cherished the way her hair flowed like
golden, brushed wheat.
He loved watching her
in her glowing radiance. He imagined

her hidden fragrance much like
the delicate bouquet of his
red wine…a cool, thin,
sweet fog eliciting an

awakening of sleeping
sensations. A spirited, scented
garland, he thought, that anoints of
anticipation.

In his myriad of thoughts she
never flinched from her gaze. Her eyes
focused. Serene. If she had ever
blinked he would not have noticed.

He wished to taste her. He held
his wine glass closer to
his lips. He craved
her sweetness. The sweetness
he was about to taste from his
red wine, an explosion of berry and
currant flavors laced with
hints of spice and soft tannins.

Suddenly, without warning his
wine glass was ripped from his hand.
"I repeat, sir, you must fasten your seatbelt.
The pilot will be landing us momentarily."

Across the center aisle of his
descending commercial aircraft
he watched his anonymous princess
dutifully close her reading book,
click her seatbelt,
adjust her seatback and folding tray
into their full upright position and
turn away to stare out her window.

And with that
the flight attendant
whisked away his
most precious and yet still
unsipped glass of red wine.

And never would he
set eyes upon it

nor her
ever again.

WATER PUDDLES

I remember, once, when I was a little boy
I walked with my dad
just the two of us
hand in hand
down a narrow country dirt road and
I remember that was the very first time
he had ever talked to me
as if I was a grown man.

It had rained all night the night before
a light rain that had turned the beaten dirt
into hard mud and filled every
blessed hole in that road
with thick, browned water…
a potholed road that now bore
more resemblance to the aftermath of a flood.

We had to walk every which way
but a straight line to avoid the myriad of pools as
he held my hand tight
as he talked and I listened
as he lead and I followed
while we stepped around puddles
he explained one of life's rules.

"You'll find soon enough for yourself," he said,
"life is a lot like these water puddles
on this here road. You have a choice
to either walk through them
or, around them," he said,
in his always carefully chosen words
in his graveled, self-confident voice.

As we walked that endless road
I asked him what if I come to a puddle that's
too wide to go around and too deep to cross.
What then?

"Then," he said,
"that'll be the time you'll have to learn to swim."

Of my life's many swimming lessons
I remember that was the very first
from my dad.

CANDLE

I loved how she knew
when I was frightened
of the night in its darkness
afraid to close my eyes and

I loved when she would come
quietly into my room
and sit on my bed
and light a candle
and tell me her stories with
such caring,
such patience, I would

put my ear to her chest
and tell her heart my
most private things, things from

my most inner world
that only she could understand
that only she should know
that only she would love
that only she knew how to
so tenderly touch
and make me
feel forever mended with her
forever love, I will

always remember how
she could make
all my fears just
fall away into sleep

I loved to hear her stories

her stories that kept me safe
from the night in its darkness
and I will always love
her smile that glowed in the
bright, fragile light
that came from her
candle.

THERE ARE TIMES

There are times
when a handshake with dad
or a hug from mom
through the telephone or in a letter
is all I need to make me back in balance
for the rest of my day.

There are times
when distant miles seem only but a
short walk to the doorstep
of loving parents who are always
waiting just outside their
open front door for whatever, whenever
I need them.

There are times
when laying on their living room floor
and the smell of their house
and the warmth of their backyard
and the feel of my old bedroom
and a fresh cup of their hot coffee
has been far, far too long in waiting.

There are times
when I am there
I am reminded of how happy I am
to share their smiling, laughing, reflecting
to be in the midst of their love, their joy
to be once again

a part of their world in which
they have unconditionally let me
come back into
for however long I want to stay.

There are times
when after he has left
their son very much wishes he could have stayed and
should have held his dad's hand a little longer and
hugged his mom a little tighter and
should have said just one more time
I love you both very much
mom and dad
if I never said that before
I want you to know that.

JUST BEFORE SUNRISE

The two children sat quietly together
just before sunrise
on their favorite park bench,
the one with their worn initials
and small heart discreetly carved
on the bench seat.

The two held each other's
hand in their laps,
as they had always done,
waiting, anticipating
the beginning of yet
another new day,
each cuddling under the
same, warm blanket and the
large, cool crown
of their tall sycamore,

a grand icon of entwined,
twisting branches painted with
dense, leathery leaves that
would soon be buzzing with
birds and butterflies prancing
with celebrations and
expectancy of what this day
was about to bring.

The two children sat quietly together
sharing their own,
innocent thoughts on the
very same park bench,
where the two of them,
now as aging grandparents,
always come to sit
loving, remembering
in those precious moments
just before sunrise.

GUARDIAN ANGEL

Guardian angel, sweet companion
don't leave my side.
I stand here, alone, in fear's mighty grip
with nowhere to run, no place to hide.

I need your strength.
The strength to throw a feather to the moon.
Stand by me, my angel, one more time
protect me that all will be well again soon.

Help me down this unknown road
no matter how narrow, no matter how wide.
Guardian angel, o' sweet companion
don't leave my side.

Veterans Day

Today is
Veterans Day.

Today is
when a country will pay tribute
to those who serve her military.
When a wife will thank
her husband for what he did and who he is.
When a son and daughter will admire
their dad for the honor he earned.
When a widow will journey
to that quiet place where her soul-mate sleeps.

It is a day
not for boasting, or bragging
nor for cheering, or celebrating
but rather for reflecting,
remembering.
Thanking those in uniform
both past and present
for the duties they performed,
the ultimate sacrifices they made
in the name of freedom
for the gratefulness of a nation
for the love of a wife
for the protection of a son and daughter.

Today will
be a day for some forgotten laughter,
some moments for a few necessary tears.
Today, time will find us standing still
at unexpected occasions
reminding us why
a wife will always
love her husband,
a son and daughter always
respect and appreciate their hero,
a widow will be placing
oh-so-carefully
a single rose upon her husband's grave.

Today is
Veterans Day.

WAITING FOR NOVEMBER

In that subconscious moment when
your capillaries slowly begin
absorbing your day's first
deep drawn breath
it is then you are assured
this is not simply
the beginnings of fall anymore.

You have been waiting and
it is finally here.

Crisp, blue-golden air
fills the soul and
rejuvenates long awaiting
inner tributaries that are
reawaking, flocking with the
swirling blackbirds and
rushing with the young
juvenile sparrows.

Today,

when you walk among the
rainbows of fallen leaves and
step around the pumpkins still
left on the ground

rejoice,

for the apples have been picked.

ME AND SALLY

I loved her.
I truly loved her.
and I know she
loved me the same
way as well. She was

either part collie and
part cocker spaniel or
part collie...and...oh well,
at the time it really didn't matter
to a nine year old.
She belonged to me and
I belonged to her and
that's all that mattered. We had

so much fun together,
running and playing...
looking out for each other. I think

there was only one time she got mad at me.
We were exploring a large
open, abandoned pasture when we
spotted a hornet's nest nestled
inside this thick, green leafed
bush intertwined with milky white
stems. Without even so much as
asking Sally, I threw a dirt clod

into the bush to see what would happen.
That was the only time I ever
ran faster than her as those
madder-than-heck hornets chased us
all the way home, all the while a
barking Sally right behind me.
For the longest time

I was convinced she had been
barking at the hornets to
leave us alone. But now
I realize the truth. During our frenzied
high paced retreat she was actually
scolding me, furiously, for getting us
both into that moronic-witted situation in
the first place.
I had never seen her
brown eyes that big before. I'll never know
who got stung more that day...
me
or Sally.
But still, she was and remained
my protector.

Soon after she had
her second litter of pups, my aunt and uncle came
into the garage to have a look at
her new clan. I had just
finished rearranging the tiny, naked
newborns so each could get at its own
nipple for milk. Suddenly my uncle
reached down and affectionately picked me
up high toward the
lower beams of the ceiling. Well, I tell you,

Sally, in a lightening flash, was up
and out of her makeshift
cardboard box bed barking at
the top of her lungs to put me down, while her
pups squirmed in total confusion. My uncle
instantly dropped me all the way
to the floor. Boy,
did that hurt. When the day came

we had to take Sally to be
put down because her cancer had
rotted her body throughout...I could
not do it. I just...could not do it. And so,
my dad ended up having to take her.
When he finally came back home
that was the very first time
I ever saw my dad cry.

But oh the sweet times we
did have. Yep. That was us.
Me and Sally.
She was my dog.
I loved her.
I truly loved her.

THE BOARD

We were about to be introduced
to the board of education.
Skippy Bryant was my bestest friend.
And we were late, again. Somehow

we could never plant in our
carefree brains that when the
school bell rang the end of recess
it was time now and not 10 minutes from now
to come back to Mrs. Flaghorn's classroom. We

always thought we had intentions to be
obedient but, perhaps from the fact
that we were obnoxious little brats
to begin with, we felt this
hostile animosity from her.
And so it was much more convenient
and fun for us to simply conclude that
we hated her guts
and therefore naturally created our own
preambled justification for coming in late.
But this, however, was our fifth offense
and this, we thought…no…knew

was pretty darned serious to find
the two of us seated in the waiting room of
the principal's office. This

was not going to be pleasant as
Skippy and I stared at his closed door. Was
he ever going to come out
or were we somehow
going to be allowed to
sweat it out for a few minutes
and that would be our lesson to us. Coming

out of his door, Mr. Johnson was holding
a flat-handled, rectangular board
that had a bunch of perfectly round holes in it.
He slapped his open palm with the board
and sternly said,
"This, boys, is the board of education.
Who's first?!"

CATCH

There was
the first time I ever hooked
my very own fish all by myself.
A heavy trout.
I was using a shiny
stainless steel triple-barbed lure.
It was my dad's.
He didn't know I had taken it. My mind

was racing so quickly.
I was going to be so proud to
show him my beautiful new catch, but
how was I going to explain that I had
caught my prize with his brand new
not even out of the box lure.
Not to fear. I wouldn't tell him
the part about using his lure. Right now

my real fear was that this
cold-blooded aquatic vertebrate
might probably snap my light line. Instead,

still fiercely leaping and gyrating
a mere few feet from where
I stood at the river's edge
the danged thing abruptly
spit loose the lure then
hastily darted back, deep into
the river's rapid depths
never to be seen again. I am

most positive my fish
must have told every other fish
in that river where I was and
what I was up to. So, after

three more hours of catching
nothing more than a sunburn
I returned the non-virgin lure back
to its box and to my dad's tackle box
in the small corner of his garage. The next
morning, at the breakfast table, dad
looked me straight in the eye
with his non-telegraphing poker face and
calmly said to me,
"He got away, didn't he?"

I tried to avoid eye contact. He then
put the box with the
new shiny lure inside it
onto the table in front of me
and said,
"This is a bass lure.
If you're going after trout
you should use a trout lure."

Right then and there
I knew exactly how
my trout, wherever it now swam, felt.
I was caught, but
I got away. Years later

I would come to realize on that
morning, at the breakfast table, I
really didn't get away with anything.
I was let go.

UBIQUITY

When the first rain
begins falling later today
will you run to your bedroom,
raise up the window and
sprawl wide onto your bed to
listen to your garden?
Listen to your mustard greens
and squash frolicking? This morning

your potatoes and turnips
felt the coming rain but did not
want to tell you
so as not to steal the thunder
from the clouds. Will you

watch your garden leaves
drink and dance and vaunt
their fragrances in the midst of
the cleansing drops? Will you

be mad when you
notice the fattened woodchuck
stealing up the corner tree with
your first, and already half eaten,
tomato of the season? In the

morning, dripping stems and
faint puddles will be all but a
whispering impression of the nightlong rain.

Won't it be wonderful

all of your senses still playing and twirling
with the brilliant bouquets and colors
coming from your fresh washed garden.

And won't it seem amazing

to think that you are a tiny, yet significant
twinkling part of your garden in all its
ubiquity.

HER EYES TOLD ME

She said not a word. Never a single word.
But her eyes…her eyes said volumes.
As if speaking only to me. It was

almost by accident I glanced her through the
crawling ants of swirling people…tourists.
She was sitting alone on top of her
checkered blanket on a pocket of flat stone.
Her legs and bare feet curled indiscriminately under her
left hip, supported solely by her
rolled-up sleeve arm. She stared

to me twenty feet across a littered walkway
on a gray, routine overcast day in
Chapultepec Park in Mexico City. Her gaze

pierced straight through
my heart. At that moment her eyes
told me her entire life. I'll never

forget she was so young, but yet she
looked so old, so withered, so beaten up by life.
Deep within her eyes she told me,
in her hunger and begging, how youthful she
once was. Beautiful. Proud. I asked

"Tienes hambre?" (Do you have hunger?)
She did not speak. But her eyes told me.
I handed her my just bought cone of mixed fruit.
"Gracias…" her faded, cracked lips motioned slowly, silently.

On that day I felt in my soul…tears.
No, I shall never forget that most gracious lady
on that day in Chapultepec Park.
The day her eyes told me…
of life.

I Must Be Getting Old

I must be getting old.
It never occurred to me until
my wife just reminded me

how I used to cook her dinner,
now she does all the cooking.
How I used to bring her breakfast in bed,
now I'm grumpy until she serves me
my morning newspaper and grapefruit.
Is this the sign of old age?

How we used to read together fine literature,
now I'm immersed in star trek reruns.
How we used to cherish our weekend getaways,
now I seem to overly describe (in detail) my
trash emptying experiences at the end of the driveway.
Am I getting old?

How I used to bring her flowers and
write beautiful poetry for her,
now I scotch tape grocery store coupons
on the side of the refrigerator for her to see.
How I used to tell her every day
I love you
now, it seems, I don't.
Have I really forgotten?

I guess I must be getting old.

WHAT I SEE

As we approached from behind
he appeared no more or less usual
than the droves of us who had flocked
to this place for the same purpose.

Today he was just one of us
and if we had taken the time
to think about it,
it was really quite amusing, all of

us like a never-ending passage of
ants assiduously flowing up and down
an allotted thin crack in a walkway
gulping unaccustomed thin air
in warm late afternoon, he and

us oblivious to the
mischievous breeze that
threatened to lift off our hats and
tumble them into a place
far below us where even the most
powerful zoom lenses that adorned
most of our necks would not
be capable of recovering.

His stride was of a
slower promenade than ours and
as we passed him we instantly became
keenly aware not to interfere with the
sweeping pattern of his
bright, red-tipped cane.

His father carefully guided him to
the waist high retaining rail of
the lookout point where we were
standing and said to him,
"This…is the Grand Canyon.
I wish you could see this."

The son did not flinch his smile.
He took his father's hand,
held it tight to his chest
and said, "I wish you could see what I see.
I love you."

THE ROCK

I kicked a rock today.
I wanted to kick it.
I honestly cannot tell you why.
For no apparent reason
I wanted to kick this...
this rock.
So I did.
It was not a very big rock.
But big enough to hurt
my naked, big toe.
A lot.

I wanted to pick it up and throw it.
I was mad. Really mad.

But before I could
the pint sized boulder want-to-be
looked up at me through its
rounded, scruffy-stoned face and said,
"Thank you for not throwing me."

I looked down at it and
at the moment I had
nothing to say to it.
My toe was beginning to throb, but
how can you stay mad
at a little rock?

So, I said it was welcome,
barely.

And the small rock continued,
"You did not hurt me when
you kicked me. But you would have
hurt my feelings if you would have
thrown me."

Oh.

From now on,
I will be more considerate
when I am walking.

PENCILS

When my mother found out
I began taking a liking to scribbling bursts of
thoughts and ideas, which were
mostly nothing more than disassembled
words that at the time could not
find purposeful function in a sentence, she

bought me a typewriter…really.
An electric typewriter complete with
keys and ribbon and sounds that
went ding and paper that obediently
rode the back of a rubber roller. She thought

I had potential?…of perhaps
becoming a future award winning
novelist and the only thought I had was
this new gadget was
the neatest thing since
sliced bread, but then mom dropped
an unsuspected bomb on me, telling me
I now had to learn how to type (uh-oh) to which
I reminded her that she, herself, was the one
who told me that wherever I go
always, always carry in my pocket a
simple notepad because no matter how
babbled a thought I may think of,
write it down…I would find a purpose for it
sometime, somewhere. But still

can you imagine how silly I must have looked
lugging that typewriter back and forth
to school, not to mention
that the thing was dang heavy? One day

I would indeed like to shake
the hand of the person who invented

pencils.

SWEATLODGE

I have beaten the drum
in the sweatlodge. I have
felt the pitch black heat of the
water and rocks. I have

felt the cleansing within the
chanting of prayer. I have seen
things in three hours of

steam and darkness that my
eyes could never see in a
whole lifetime. Was it

Grandfather's wisdom that
opened me during those
times of purifying and song? Was it

the blessing of the
tobacco that brought us
closer, at least for then, to

a truth we could only touch
within the confines of a
tipi? I swear I was

almost there. But,
not quite. For,
I have beaten the drum
in the sweatlodge.

FLOYD

Floyd was cool.
He was like my second dad, only, well…
you know, like the dad you could tell stuff to
that you would not tell your own dad.
Like the dad that would tell me stuff that
my own dad never did.

I remember my brother and I were small kids
when he moved into the house
right across the dirt street from ours.
He and dad hit it right off.
But with Floyd and me
there was something I would like to believe
that made our bond more allied.

From his tall, skinny frame and his
pointed, zigzag jaw and his
last remaining front buck teeth came
a constant churn of humor and
infectious laughter and his face
was an identical twin of an
eternally jovial, paternal burro.
But he was my happy burro and
I took affection to these things about him, except…
I preferred to keep all my teeth.

And I very often preferred he'd not used his
clinching vice grip every time he
shook my hand but I came to reason that
this was his way of hugging me and
there was not much chance of my hand
suffering any degree of permanent damage.

The day we buried his wife, Marge, was the
only day I ever saw him buckle to his knees and
the only time his hands turned to mush.
It was Floyd's hands that showed me how to

pick a sun ripe, big beef tomato from his
backyard vine and devour it right there
on the spot with help from a salt shaker.
He taught me how to fly his airplane and
his wise horse sense illustrated
the difference between those of
patience and perceptiveness and
those who will forever be
picking at straws while trying
to build a brick house.

I let him down only once.
One morning while sitting at his kitchen table
I wanted so bad to beat him at cards
I cheated. He caught me. Without saying a word
he quietly stood up and walked out
into the sanctuary of his back yard.
I had never felt hurt in my heart
like that until then. Not too long after
he forgave me
with an extra hard hug of his handshake.

Over time his chain smoking allowed
his cancer to wither his body to
a stick of driftwood. And even in his final days
his hazel-green eyes were never of
failure or resentment.

The last time I saw him was in an obscure hospice
in an empty part of town and he
said to me, as he had often stubbornly said
"You know the old saying 'you can't take it with you'
has never been proven.
And right now I ain't willing to test it."

He was like my second dad.
I loved him.
Floyd was cool.

FROM YOUR BALCONY

The chickens know better.
They know to get out early if
they wish to get the first specklings of
nearby grains and worms, and of course
delight in the fact they will not lose even
one cluck of henhouse gossip,
keeping them far too occupied to
pay any attention to the

hummingbirds, already
darting and buzzing, joyfully
dipping their dark tongues into
cool water tranquilly bubbling from
the front yard marbled fountain while

a young rooster stretches his neck
and flaunts his spiked, red comb
to officially announce,
again and again and again,
the cool beginnings of
another hot, dry morning, unaware

the hummingbirds have
reluctantly begun retreating as
starlings zoom in one at a time under
the cloak of their black feathers
to come drink their fill and as

you watch, with some slight
amusement, you are mindful
not to be angry with the starlings
because you know this is
how it is and resolve to simply

enjoy the delicious fragrances
wafting from nearby groves of
almonds and plums and
the sweet, dry grass across
the graveled driveway, beaconing
your knees to run out and frolic
with the new day, but not until
you have finished enjoying your coffee.
Life is good. Let the day begin
from your balcony.

THE MONARCH AND THE CROW

The days grow longer
from the cold winter that
unwillingly starts to let go.

The monarch gathers itself.

It is strong
it has survived winter's rule
it flies
it is time.

Long and northward
it flies gracefully, softly, rhythmically
to ensure the survival of
its others, for it will not.
This will be its second and
last migration.

The shiny, black young crow
darts and weaves
so ever impatiently, mischievously
all around the high flying monarch.
It taunts the old butterfly
disrespectfully, persistently.

"If you must eat me be done with it.
For I must make it to the milkweed
and I still have a long way to go
and I am weary and your nasty tongue
irritates me. Your non intelligent eyes
show me no respect and you stink of something dead,"
the monarch arrogantly flapped in the crows face.

Till now, this is something
the young crow had not yet been taught.
And it had not been shown how to apologize.
And while it jerks its head with
indecision, confusion
the old monarch turns to
continue its journey and silently smiles and
does not look back.

SPARROW

I had never tried so hard
to wish for a young bird to
fly

to lift herself from the cold dirt path
where she sat motionless
looking confused…dazed?…and
like you, being of good Samaritan,
I had to ask her if
she was hurt in which

she silently turned her head
away from me in which

I said to her that it appeared
she had molted into feathers
healthy enough to fly in which

she then turned completely
away from me and so

I pinched off a small crumb
from the cookie in my shirt pocket and
tossed it before her in which

she quickly hopped over and
plucked it into her beak and abruptly
flew away
into the safety of a
tall walnut tree and
I swear I could see her smiling as she
flew away
with her delicious prize in which

I said
glad I could help,
precious little sparrow

now

go home

where is your mother?

MOTHER'S DAY

When you reflect upon today
embrace this day as a time for
remembering
all of the wonderful, caring, loving moments
your mother caressed you
with her love for you.

Remembering
how mother first awakened and nurtured you
into a most wondrous new world that
no matter what happened, she
would always be there for you.

Remembering
when you left her nest to be
a grown-up on your own
mother hugged you even tighter
to her heart, you were never really alone.

Remembering
how much mother has made you
what you are and always will be
to everyone and everything that you
touch in this world we call planet earth.

Remembering
she thinks about you every day
she waits for you on this day because
today, above all other days, this is her day
for today…is mother's day.

DADS AND RADISHES

It was always fascinating
watching such a thing
before our very eyes
at first light while waiting
for the promise of a soon to be

warm sun about to rise over
the glass-smooth water
the dark air biting our lips and lungs.
No one else around. Just me

and my brother
and my dad
sitting motionless
in our cramped, tiny aluminum boat
rocking smack dab in the middle
of Shaver Lake shivering with
anticipation while inhaling
thick gas fumes still
stubbornly clinging to us
after the sputtering outboard motor
was shut down. It was

always an education
watching dad rigging up our
poles and lines
tying the various knots
and meticulously attaching
those flat, shiny trawling spoons. And, I

guess it just wouldn't be fishing
without the smell of old,
crusted jars of
salmon eggs permeating from
dad's oft' repaired rusting
tiered tackle box. Forget about
the two hours ago
when dad had to impatiently
stop his old pick-up truck
alongside the twisting mountain road
so that my brother and I could
do our business
from being car sick but
right now all that mattered were
magical thoughts of
record breaking trout
dangling from our stingers
at the end of the day while
watching dad
working his fishing magic
and each of us sharing from
the same sandwich bag filled with
back-yard grown radishes
dad had picked and
brought for our breakfast.

HAPPINESS IS MY WARM BATHROBE

I think it is one of the
most perfect unions
ever devised, especially
when the cold nights
come, and I

will tell you that
when this liaison ensues there is
no sweeter bass hum than
the innocuous rhythm of
greased bearings and rollers
dutifully spinning a
cylindrical drum tasked with
the mission of moving high heat
around and through
my fuzzy, perfectly weighted
cotton bathrobe, tumbling in

3-quarter time, patiently awaiting
the buzzing of my electric dryer's
30-minute timer, when then
my robe will
adorn me with
incubating warmth
penetrating me, permeating me
beyond my goose-bumped flesh,
beyond my aching bones,
down to my wooly slippers
purring with me in
total agreement that

there is no greater working bond
between machine
and thread,
between my electric dryer
and my terry cloth cotton bathrobe.

Happiness is my warm bathrobe.

Except tonight.

I hate electric power outages…

Farmer's Market

It has been said
food is the international language for peace.
What a wonderful thought and
how so very true.

In our tucked away town of El Segundo,
Thursday night market goes on
every week, come rain or shine when
the city maintenance trucks
respectfully cordon off main street between
idly blinking red lights.

It is quite official, with the required permits and
all of the other etceteras of
necessaries, obligatories and requisites
shoved dutifully into the glove compartments
of the faithful, old farm trucks converging from
as far away as Fresno and San Luis Obispo.

Here you will not find the likes of
any big corporate growers with
supermarket intentions…oh no…this is
meant strictly for the small, privately owned
farmer who humbly comes to
sell his peace offerings.

Only at Thursday night market can you
do the slow mosey down the middle of your
temporary haven of wonderful aromas,
tantalizing smells and crisp, fresh
produce that is nothing short of eye candy.
There is really no finer place to be when one is
in search of honest, wholesome food and

the very latest free gossip.

Let's talk…
Dinner will wait…

So Bee It

I never knew for sure if
        a honeybee can not swim
        or can.

But just now I learned firsthand how
        it showed me, then told me
        it can't.

In a small, quiet pool I just saw that
        no matter how much it tried to swim or float
        it couldn't.

It kicked and it stroked and fought hard not to drown
        so determined to fight death off and so far
        it did.

Though its pleas were silent it called for my help and
        though I feared it might sting my rescuing hand
        it didn't.

So instantly fragile and motionless it had become
        I wanted so hard for it to live and somehow knew
        it would.

It shivered and fluttered to regain its life and
        as it twitched in my palm I thought it still might die but
        it wouldn't.

So I asked it, "When you stopped to drink did you see how deep
the water was and remember to be careful?" She said yes,
she had.

"Did you know that the nectar you just gathered is very heavy on
your tiny legs, making it hard to fly?" She said no,
she hadn't..

She explained that she was excited of her new nectar find and so
anxious to do her victory dance to all the bees at her hive
she forgot.

With a grateful buzz she lifted to the sky, off to her hive and
though I will miss this tiny honeybee, before she is even
home, of me she will have already
forgotten.

PRINCIPLES

Drawing to an inside straight
was one of those dispiriting lessons
recurrently drilled into me
by my dad as
having little or no chance of
occurring when indulging in
the gamely art of
5 card stud. But then,

I would think,
"What the hell,"
and argue to him that
as good fortune
will at times have it
it can happen. Nevertheless

this was dad
who lived by such
quiet principles such as
never allowing himself
to be influenced by
a long shot or the underdog.
He was always
so damned practical
not to mention
set-your-clock-by-it predictable
and for the most part
somewhat tolerant. On the

flip side
there was mom.
Always equilaterally

open minded
not to mention
to-a-fault forgiving
and for the most part
had the patience of an angel. For the

longest time I would ask myself,
"How did they do it?"
Both at times poles apart in their ways
and yet so perfectly bonded
in marriage, and yes
even in most principles. In time,
I grew to understand that
although their marriage
may not have been
perfectly chiseled in stone
it was no longer this
riddle wrapped up
in a mystery. And so,

perhaps with
my own share of
fortune, patience,
understanding and love
a few of these principles
from each of them
might possibly
replicate themselves in me,
if I am so lucky. But then

as good fortune
will at times have it
it can happen.
It can happen.

MESTIZO

It looks so badly cracked
       and old, but it is acutely steady,
       the hand of the young mestizo
       that reaches an over-ripe papaya
       just above my bound wrists
       to my face
       barely beyond the end
       of the barrel of his M-16 rifle.
       He motions for me to take a bite.
The young Honduran's pot-marked
       face wears of an awkward
       fresh honor, loyalty
       and relief
       that he has not yet been told
       to kill us.
       His right sandal strap is worn, almost broken.
       His lips cock an
       unpretentious stare.
Gritty damp, and cool
       almost slick
       is the strange feel of this
       mountain dirt, mud
       under our sprawled legs and butts,
       while us four Americanos
       can only now presume
       what the chairs waiting for us
       at the embassy in Tegucigalpa
       should be feeling like.
       Right now, I am feeling cold.
       My brain tries to escape.

Back to thoughts of the curving
>	Rio Choluteca
>	we had flown across
>	just before our pilots and the third
>	one with the missing two front teeth
>	took our plane down
>	to this fertile plateau strip and
>	their waiting comrades.
>	And here we wait. And tremble. And listen
>	to Spanish being spoken quietly, privately
>	by the ones holding the guns and
>	smoking the non-filtered cigarettes.
>	Are they still deciding
>	what to do with us? Perhaps. We wait.
My dry mouth has instantly absorbed
>	the rich juice
>	from my one bite of the papaya.
>	I try to take
>	another bite
>	but my young captor stingily pulls the fruit
>	back
>	behind the trigger of his rifle
>	and then proceeds
>	to devour the rest of it
>	in front of me
>	his eyes frozen upon me
>	while he slowly chews.
I am feeling the grip of desperation
>	tighten around my throat and chest
>	and I begin to beg to my young captor .

"Did not we pay you
        in good faith
        the lempira
        you and your airplane wanted
        to get us to our embassy?"
        I say in
        half broken Spanish and
        half broken English.
        I think that I should
        apologize for not being
        more eloquent in
        his native tongue
        but I know what I have just spoken
        will work.
I wait for the mestizo
        to answer
        but
        he turns his head
        to the El hefe in charge
        to which the El hefe answers
        with an old Honduran saying
"Un bien con un mal se paga"
(a good deed is repaid with a bad one.)
The mestizos all laugh
        but I
        I understand!

Journey

They appear as
pinpoints in the sky
growing larger as they
approach.
Do you see them?

The seagulls do not,
always too frantic
scavenging for whatever the
sea and sand discard.

The mother otter knows
when they are here but
always too focused
surviving, showing
her pup how to feed himself.

But yet, each late afternoon
they come

gliding, swaying
straight along the beach and surf
to the rhythm of the air.
Winged sentries in V-formation
suspended high in thin wisps of
air streamed fog and clouds. And then

swooping down, they skim low
keeping barely a feather's reach
ahead of green tube curls.
What fun! Are they

smiling as they
dance and flirt
with the breakers? Do they

delight with amusement
riding up and over the
closing white churn?

And then
suddenly, up high they go
rising swiftly on
wafted salt thermals
of drafts and currents
once again
watching, guarding
wing tip to wing tip they

keep going, unwavering
in their resolve to get to where
they must go.

The mother otter hands her pup
a crustacean she has just
cracked open for him.
She does not look up. Yet
she knows…

the pelicans
are going home. But
they will be back
tomorrow.

ONE OF THOSE DAYS

Cold wet air
gray lifeless overcast sky
the last fingers of frost still on the front lawn
      thermostat on 73
         chalk pastels on the living room carpet
         a low, slow fire caressing the inner walls of the fireplace
            it seems to be one of those days.

E-mail to send
the last sip of cold hot chocolate
an empty box of detergent next to a pile of laundry
      an old forgotten song on LP
      a cat named Spot rolling on her back
      a just turned 40 birthday card rediscovered (oh my)
         it seems to be one of those days.

Laughing with you
flipping through our wedding album
reading back through our honeymoon book we wrote
      you holding me
      making up our grocery list
      looking for our mailbox key
         it seems
         I love these kinds of days.

NEEDLE

Late last night,
during the power outage,
while sewing in
the living room
my wife was reminded just
how rusty she had become
with the art of needle and thread
when she involuntarily
flicked her needle
(saved by the thimble)
onto the rug...
somewhere.

Guided only by the
soft luminance
from the fireplace
we chaotically tried to find it but...
didn't.

Early this morning,
on my sojourn to the kitchen
my right big toe abruptly
found it.

Ouch...

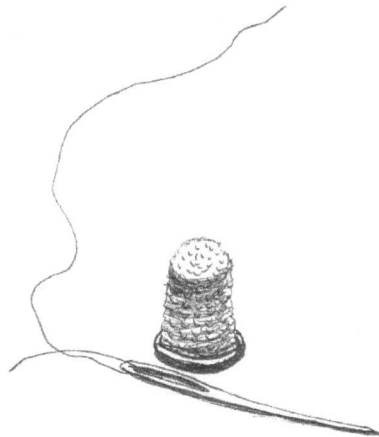

Song

This evening
warm, sweet velvet air
gently cleanses her in supple waves.

A camouflaged cricket
proclaims a solo concerto from
just behind tall, weaving reeds that
hug the last of this day's
soft blush of muted, rusting light.

A dragonfly brushes near and
whispers to her then
dances on the clear glass surface
of the cool water.

The first twinkling stars
are casting their blanket of
radiant comfort.

Her delicate wings
joyfully pulse in eurhythmic dance
to a most gentle air brush that is
but a faint whisper.

Oh, how she is glowing
tenderly hugging
her very own silk petal.
She is once again
youthful and safe.

She is at her
secret, tucked away pond.
She has arrived.

The butterfly has come home.

THE NIGHT

Stars flicker high above
the Sonoran desert on a
dry, bitter cold night.

The tangy whiff of the small
mesquite campfire hangs in the
still, biting air.

In the distance, a lone coyote calls and
from the foothills comes an
answering yip.

The night has now come
a third time to the young Navajo,
alone in his journey of cleansing.
He yearns for the incubating warmth of
the sweatlodge,
his smoking smudge stick,
tightly bound sage and juniper,
smells sweet
as he purifies himself with it.

Tonight, the young Navajo
prays for purity and guidance
before taking his vows when
the sun is highest tomorrow.
Into the night he prays for
wisdom from his ancient ancestors,
the Anasazi.

And in the hollow, frigid air of
the night

the lone coyote calls.

The lone coyote calls.

TOMATO

I would like to be in my next life…a tomato.
I thought about it, and yes I could perhaps be
a great philanthropist. Or,
a bald eagle soaring amongst clouds. Or,
maybe a carefree bottlenose dolphin
surfing with the sunfish. Or,
even a new water fall
(size does not matter) somewhere. No,
I would want more. I would

want to be craved…and loved…and desired.
I would be total tomato.
Unconditionally, unreservedly your
Big Beef
Early Girl
Better Boy, or
Cherry, or
Roma.
I would delight your garden.
Your taste buds would
spring about your senses
with each taste of me, while my
sweet juice oozes down your chin. I would

be your one, true innocent pleasure.

You would want me and
pluck me and
hold me and
squeeze me and
savor me and
of course desire more of me
salt shaker or not. And in

return I would be plumpingly happy
knowing I am the one thing
you crave that can offer zero calories with
no guilt trip. And so

you can just
bite me…and I will sing you my
luscious fragrances till the end of my season
knowing it's just you and me, and

a box of miracle grow.

BISCUITS

When I was a kid
a sloppy hot dog on
a plain paper plate
was just the
next row back from heaven
but that did not stop
mom from always
placing onto our laps
her best dinner napkins.

I heard my mother say it
more than once
"Keep it simple
but add just a touch
of elegance."

Mom was like that.

Dad. Well, dad was
focused in other directions
like trying to show me how to
throw a baseball
catch a football
teach me how to
properly fish and not
snap his new fishing line while
trying to unsnag his
last expensive lure.

I admit I didn't always
give it my best. One day I realized
he knew that.

Still…dad never gave up.

I heard my father say it
more than once
and I have remembered it
a hundred times since.
"If ya throw an old boot in the oven
don't expect to pull out biscuits."

I am still working on his recipe for biscuits.

Honor Guard

Honor guard, honor me
this one last time.

Stand by me, in your solemn attention
fixed three to each side, command your
white gloves to carry me my final steps
to my eternal, silent place.
I salute you.

I salute you, for I have seen you
standing proudly in the
summer's heat, the winter's cold,
your heads bowed in silent prayer
for all soldiers, young and old
most of whom you never knew
but yet know so well.
I thank you.

I thank you, for so freely giving
your task, so rich in tradition,
forged in honor and accepting of
nothing less than excellence. And
although we come from all walks of life,
we will always share the common bond of
having had a humbling experience and
a high privilege.
I honor you.

I honor you for being here for me,
for those I leave behind and
for all those you will remember that
follow me for yours is a never ending duty
because the post of honor is a
forever private station.
With the single crack of your rifles
I pass the mantle and the torch.
You know this to be your charge,
always reminded of this each time you
extend the folded flag knowing the
only thing harder than being a soldier…
is loving one.

Honor guard, honor me
this one last time.

SPANISH RICE

She looked of lavender
she smelled of lavender
I remember it like yesterday.

On one particular day I had
forgotten my bag lunch.
So on that day I chose
to sit apart from my companions.

To my surprise she
came and sat down right next to me,
smoothing out her dress.
She said a couple of cheerful words to me.
At the moment I didn't hear what she said.

I remember she
smelled so pretty.
As pretty as she looked.
She offered me something
from her small rose colored
metal lunch box.

A tiny portion of rice
(she had divvied her portion in half).
It was good.
She said it was called Spanish rice.
She said it was her favorite.
I believe from that moment on
it became my favorite as well.

And then there was the time
when I had walked to my best friend's house
(about a mile away).
And I had just begun to walk back home when
in her car, she pulled up alongside of me
and offered me a ride home. Naturally I said yes.
At the time I didn't care

where she was taking me, she was
simply taking me somewhere.

Me…with her…in her car…together.
It just couldn't have been better.
Me…alone…with her.
And I even let her
drive a couple of blocks
past my house just so I could
be with her a little longer.
My, oh my.
Just the two of us in her car.
When we stopped, as I
opened the door to get out, she said,
"Did you know I'm getting married?"
I was shattered.

After what seemed like forever
I was able to clear my throat
to ask who it was.
She said, very caringly,
"I'm getting married to Mr. Jamison.
He's the 4th grade teacher here at
Wolters Elementary school. Think of it.
In two more years you'll be
in his class."

And so it was
on that day…at that moment…in my
7th year of existence I found out from
my 2nd grade teacher, Miss Cornet, that she
was giving herself to another man.

Yes, I suppose I shall always
remember her.
She looked so lovingly of lavender
she smelled so sweetly of lavender
and I loved her…Spanish rice.

LIFE BEGINS AT FIFTY

Mark Twain once wrote
The older I get, the better I used to be.
I am beginning to believe
there just may be a
hint of truth to his hindsight, cause
I never thought I'd see the day
when I'd meekly mutter to my own self
let alone even try to believe it,
life begins at fifty.

I would like to believe that
life, for me, begins at fifty.
Despite the fact that
by then everything else on me is
starting to wear out, fall out and spread out
provoking anticipated thoughts that
are, quite frankly, not at all so nifty.

I would like to think the adage
"the best is yet to come" is still a sure-fire bet.
Although, to the best of my knowledge
or, so I've been told, there are
three signs of becoming fifty.
The first is your loss of memory,
the other two…I forget.

Would it be too assuming
to accept "golden years" as a perk?
When I think back on all the things
I used to do, be able to do, think I can still do
I am beginning to realize that
I have, by now, put much more credence in
"work is a lot less fun and
fun a lot more work."

Yes, I will indeed admit
most of my youth has yielded to middle age.
I've long since stopped growing at both ends
and now only seem to be growing in the middle.
Caution is just about the only thing I care to exercise,
I am finding it takes longer to rest than to get tired.
Yep, I guess I must be turning fifty, all right,
my receding hairline is my constant gauge.

I would like to believe there is some
preponderance to this
life begins at fifty…thing.
Although I was assured that
I would experience such a
sensation at twenty,
see stars at thirty,
bask in neon lights at forty.
It seems now at fifty I am still waiting, if you know what I mean.

But I will not give up, for
it is here I must find my truth.
Therefore I shall yield…and join the **F.I.F.T.Y.** club
and proudly proclaim

F.ifty
I.s
F.ine
T.uning
Y.outh

MOCKINGBIRD

How amazing,
watching clusters of sparrows quickly
collecting themselves in mid-air
searching for the first earthworms and snails
of the new day and when there are
none to be found how swiftly they

begin pirouetting and somersaulting
in perfect synchronization
into a nearby eucalyptus to pick
what nectar and seeds are left
only to find the seed pods already
opened and empty,
scattered upon the ground.
The finches had beaten them to it.

The mockingbird was having fun
with all this.
She was watching them.
And she was watching me
and I could hear her.

Before I had hopped over the
thin slivered brook,
before I had gotten past the
rows of strawberries,
or even past the eucalyptus
she began singing her
chortled songs, her
hazy, blue feathers concealed behind
bright green leaves sprouting
from a slender fig branch.

She saw me coming, but I could not,

or perhaps I did not want to,
see her or even look for her because
my purpose was to pick
the sweet figs that were
plump and puffing their
morning purple chests
practically shouting to me to
hurry and put them in my basket
before the raccoons and possums
came for them.

The young mockingbird
sang endlessly, pouring all of her
color and personality into melody,
triumphantly caroling
that her babies had already
eaten their fig feast and were about
to take their very first flight.

I delighted in her victory and
her tree filled with figs.

And when my basket was full and
after I had gotten back
past the eucalyptus and
past the rows of strawberries and
hopped back over the brook,

the mockingbird

was still singing.

SNAIL

I wanted to simply sit and be quiet,
alone…and touch the damp earth
and plants with my fingers when
I noticed a diminutive, brownish snail
next to my hand looking up at me.
She wished to introduce herself.

I said,
"Are you talking to me? I never met
a snail before, let alone talk to one."

She said,
"But you would like me,
cause I like what I am, and
I get to eat green, healthy stuff, and
I'm kinda cute, and
I'm kinda slow, and,
at least I'm not a slug."

Hmm…she had a point.
I said, "Okay…"

She continued…
"I, at least, I have a shell.
Did you know I am called,
among a few other things,
escargot by
Sir duck and Lord jaybird and Count snake?
I am constantly being invited to dinner.
Just ask

loads of toads and
hurdles of turtles
and the beetles and the chickens
and don't forget the geese.
It's so nice to be so wanted when you are
someone...er...some**thing**, like me.

I am *Helix aspersa*. Kinda catchy, ain't it?

Now that we've introduced ourselves
I already like you, therefore you may simply
call me
            snail."

THE TWO OLD MEN

It was their favorite time of day.
It was their favorite place to be.
The two old men would always sit
at the same, sand beaten table on the
low dune at the beach,
at first sharing a few
oft repeated stories of
embellished adventures and
past friendships but then
mainly memories of their wives. And when

they talked they seldom would take
their gaze from the tossing surf for chance
their eyes might reveal within themselves
a concealed emotion that must
remain shielded. They were

two old men bonded by lonesomeness,
the rolling sea their solace.
One shared his past happiness, the other
mostly his long sadness. Their stories

offered between them
perhaps some soothing, perhaps healing
as if mending loose ends of faded
pieces of significance in their lives that
each had misplaced and could not find. Yet for

the both of them their cast had been
unwittingly set long ago, like
the predestined settings of a shallow tide pool,
who the lucky one was who had touched true love and
the one who had mated but never found such meaning.
One wishing, and the other one not
to do it over again. The splinters

of that salted beach table have grown longer now
where the tides still dutifully transfuse the nearby sands,
where sacred talks and precious memories
once thrived on that little stretch of shore
where the waning sun would hit
at the old broken table
where the two old men
used to sit.

SLAPPING TORTILLAS

My mother would send me to school with
sliced apples and cold sandwiches enclosed in
layers of plastic wrap.
Marco's mother would send him with
cut jicama and warm tortillas wrapped in
bits of tin foil.

When we got to school
it was a good trade.

After school,
we often would walk home together
arriving at Marco's house first, where
the yummy aroma of Mexican cooking
wafted throughout his small-squared,
blue adobe dwelling with an aproned
Mrs. Lopez greeting us
near the door telling us we were just in time,
instructing us to wash our hands
then pulling us into her tiny, compact kitchen.

On floured sheets of waxed paper
there would be a couple dozen, or so,
rolled balls of dough waiting to be
formed into rounded flats of tortillas and
Marco and I would each be issued
a tray of dough and ushered out
onto the thinly shaded, back porch to
shape tortillas with our hands.

When our hands got busy, we
gave no thought as to where his
three older sisters were, always too occupied
doing what growing girls do.

Nor to his father, who left
two years ago to find work in the
Coachella Valley and had not yet
come back.
We were happy helping Mama Lopez
prepare supper for her family.

She wasted no time grabbing
our tortillas from us and plopping them into
two, heated cast iron skillets where they would
puff with these beautiful brown spots and
smell so out of this world and then
cover them with a clean dish towel so that
the steam would keep them warm.

She would smile and say to us,
"Una casa con tortillas es una casa feliz."
(A house with tortillas is a happy house)
and then give us each a warm tortilla with
a large thimble of melted butter and
proclaim to the world,
"Si usted puede cantar, hacerlo."
(If you can sing, do it.)

Marco and I would look to each other
and we couldn't help but laugh that
this was not a time for singing.

We were much too busy
playing and giggling and together
slapping tortillas.

I KNOCKED ONLY ONCE

The darkness
was just beginning its infancy.
The dripping, cool air
tightened around my tired bones.
But my pain was not
of the body. The forgotten

sight of the tangled thicket
of eucalyptus comforted my journey.
It had been a long time.
They were still here. Still here

refusing to yield to
faded frozen years.
Still faithfully standing over
her now brittle and
splintered shack. The patch

of garden that once grew
roses so vibrant and alive
with color had now faded into
a borderless blotch of
unkempt dirt that waited
no more for new life.

In a sunken corner
just to the side of the house
a maple tree,
her favorite,
now shriveled with drooping limbs,
protected what appeared to be
a small, weathered wooden cross.

My brain began beating with
emotion that my heart could
not shield against.

I could not be sure.
I could only…

I knocked only once.
Then, bade the darkness
and her farewell.

GRAPEFRUIT

Given that my breakfast before me was always
Ripe and red and so inviting
And even tantalized of a slight, tart aroma that my senses were
Perfectly in harmony with
Especially beginning my day, I cherished that it came
From my mother's sweet gentleness and passion and
Respect for all the simple basics and pleasures that we
Understood were the very essences of life itself and
It did not matter however the rest of the world might be, because
This was my mother's way of saying love…with a grapefruit

Teaching

What would I do
if you were not with me to
teach me to walk
the paths lined with
briars and tall, thick pines
that crest and loop at the
top of the ridge
where the stellar-jays
talk all day?

What would I do
if you were not with me to
teach me what it is like
to stand at the edge
of our ocean knee deep
in salt water at low tide
skipping over burrowing sand crabs
with our bare toes?

What would I do
if you were not with me to
tell me about
the flowers and
the bees and
the birds and
the trees that
turn our walks
into adventures?

Teach me the words to
the songs the robin sings
and I will show you
how I write my poetry.

Show me how you want
your poetry written for you
and I will write till there is no paper left.

TULE FOG

The first, cold tule fog has come in tonight.
One full day after a much needed
cleansing rain…it has come.
You can count on it.
It is here.
It does not sift in on
the back of a passing wind, not even
a slight draft. It silently

crawls in along the ground.
It does not sneak up behind you,
but all around you and
greets your face with a
penetrating dampness that is
quite deafening to your bones. Once you

have stood within the cocoon of
this sterile pea soup you will
not forget what it is like, nor
what it feels like. When I was

a boy my uncle told me on a
particularly brisk early evening
not to go wandering out.
His ranch was nestled among
many small creeks
splattered everywhere with
tule reeds (we called them cattails). But my

purpose in life at that time was
to explore. And disobey. I remember
I was near the cows…somewhere, when
the tule fog ambushed me. I must have
walked in small, disoriented circles for
at least a short forever.
Then I heard the cowbell.
The cows were walking back to
the barn behind the house. I closely
followed the sound of that
cowbell all the way back to
a worried uncle waving a
misted lit flashlight.
Only then did I realize how
startlingly chilled I had gotten. No, you
may not recall your
first encounter with tule fog
but you will always remember
what it is like to be wrapped in it.
I can only shake my head with a
conceding smile at the way
nature, in her inherent ways,
ushers in this gray vacuum
that offers, in its silent way,
a secluded domain of
soundless comfort. It will

be gone by tomorrow mid-morning.
But for now, it is here.
The first, cold tule fog has come in tonight.

Daylight Savings Time

It arrives like
a falling maple leaf,
floating gently away from
its mother branch to waiting
tepid soft soil.

The afternoons especially seem to
hug you with rediscovered
warmth and brightness.
The winter is retreating
to the north and
here, where you are,
it feels good to
open your face to the sun and

watch the tree limbs
relishing with new blossoms
and early fruit.
Your mind is leaping with
expectancy and tugs
at your body to join
the celebration of a new spring.
But where to start?

This morning
a bright, new flower was born
and it is close by
waiting to greet you.

It is time for you to
go there and
introduce yourself to it.

WINTER'S CALLING

Have you ever wondered what it is like
        to walk on fresh, powdered snow
                around and across tall pines and meadows?

Did you ever wonder how it must feel
        to be in cold, crisp air so bright
                you thought you had a chance to touch the sun?

Have you ever imagined
        the sheer exhilaration of
                gliding atop nature's perfect white fluffy carpet?

There is a magical winter world
        waiting for you
                anxious to show you her snowy cathedral.

So come grab your
        cross country skis and long poles.
        I have been there and I will show you.

SOUTH DAKOTA

My uncle Bill absolutely could not
carry a tune in a bucket.
Once a week, when he sang
at his small church in Jefferson
the people alongside him
tithed a little extra
to avoid any guilt feelings when
quietly slipping out the back door
to escape his singing. But oh

how that man could
make such sweet music
with a crop of dirt.
He could grow just about anything
on that tiny corner of South Dakota.
If ever there was a love affair between
man and soil
as a young boy I swear
I bore witness to it. He was

a farmer's farmer.
From the first fresh-tilled earth
sifting carefully through his fingers
at planting time to
glistening chaffs of wheat
springing from the palms of his hands
at harvest season, farming was
what he lived and loved.
His tall, bright green corn
proudly smiled upon him when
he walked their rows.
The rich, sweet fragrance of his
chlorophylled soy beans caressed
every awareness of your body.

And, rhubarb for supper...oh my. Everyone

loved him. Aunt Clarice loved him. I loved him.
And he loved sharing and giving
to those around him and
no one or any one part of his ground was
more important than another.
That was just how he was. He was
what God wanted him to be and
it was all he ever wanted to do.
And South Dakota was
where he belonged. Before dawn

he would be milking the cows and
working his magic with
cantankerous machinery and
temperamental tractors and then
work all day in his fields.
After tending his animals and with
just enough light left in the day to
drive a last Band-Aid nail into his
aging barn he'd slowly make his way
back to the house and quietly
close the back screen door to
the service porch next to the kitchen. Boots off,

he would exhale a long breath
from the pain of tractor-back while
aunt Clarice would take his hat and
sit him at her table.
Together they would softly
hold each other's hand and
bow their heads and
give thanks for

all they were blessed with and
uncle Bill would gently smile
for he was grateful to God for
having allowed his wife and
his land to harvest his heart. All the

people who knew him and
many of those who did not
gathered at his small church in Jefferson
to say a final goodbye to uncle Bill
on that clear, bitter cold Friday and
bury him next to aunt Clarice. They all

cried and they sang and they
were sure he was
singing right alongside them but
this time not one of them
slipped out the back door
because, you see, they all
loved this old farmer.
He was and always will be
a farmer's farmer.

THE PERFECT DAY

I love it when it's your day off
      just you and me and no plans
            snuggling an extra hour

I love when we walk at a low tide
      the smell of salt air
            our footprints in the sand

I love for us to sit in front of our fireplace
      sharing a shag carpet
            cozying in our warmth

I love how we love our old grandfather clock
      its gentle wisdom of time
            its melodic quarter hour chimes

I love when we ride in our old pick up
      going to somewhere for no reason
            not wanting the sound of the radio

I love being at our favorite spot at sunset
      the sun slowly dipping beneath the waves
            the ending of a perfect day

I love

    you

CONTINENTAL BREAKFAST

Being a boy scout, for example,
was a pain in the ass.

The very notion of
enlisting in scout hood was
I assure you never my idea
but rather mandated as
a parent requirement
in yet another
tactical attempt to
get me out of the house
to which

subsequently,
I was involuntarily
pressed into the service of
local troop 3707
at a time in my life I
defiantly regarded as
another assault upon my sprouting
adolescent independence
wherein

consequently,
I vowed not the least
interest nor intention
whatsoever of advancing beyond
the inductee rank of tenderfoot
let alone procuring even a
single merit badge
therefore

accordingly,
my brief career as a scout
was about as expressionless as
a crudely assembled
glazed figure
typically displayed at
an unrefined
house of wax museum.

I would
have only to offer that
I was not
born a habitual rebellious bastard
nor a hardened hater of
one of America's beloved
youth organizations.

I simply
never had any desire of
pledging myself
or any part thereof
to an anything that
wasn't first my idea.

And even though
my determined foundation
eventually proved successful in
getting me dismissed from
local troop 3707

I would
come to realize

my self-imposed
Neanderthal non-compliance policy
did not always serve my best interest.

On the day I walked away
from troop 3707
my scout leader,
finally yielding he was not about to
change my basic feast or famine pattern,
offered this:

You travel down your road
and at the end of the day
you come across a
one-coat-of-paint motel that
just happens to be offering
the next morning
a simple, but free, continental breakfast.
Stop. Be thankful and remember
don't be looking in the backyard for
4-leaf clovers when
opportunity comes knocking
at your front door.

Enjoy your breakfast.

THOUGHTS OF DAD

Dad would always rise early.
I always loved that.
I sometimes wonder if
this came from the
time he spent in the military or
this was just something
he loved to do. At the time

it didn't matter because
while mom was still sound asleep
I had dad all to myself and
cool mornings
that welcomed a sunrise filled with
promising expectancy. In those young

moments we did not say much.
We did not have to.
Words were not needed
between us. Dad's home was

his castle and I was one of his
loving subjects.
His backyard was his court
and I,
I was his loyal servant who
shared with him those
intimate things that could only be
shared with a father. He would often

pick an awakening flower and have me
take it to my mother and she would
graciously thank me for it.
But she knew it came from dad.
And I understood. And I was

happy because I knew
I was blessed to have
both my mom and my dad.

Dad would always rise early.
I always loved that.
I will always love my dad.

THREE DAYS IN THE SUN

A brown juvenile seagull
flies his starfish off a rock jetty
skimming barely above
dark blue rolling waves
into the last rays of sunset for
tonight's dinner.

His brothers and sisters chaotically
chase after him for his spoils.

Just on the other side of
the foaming breakers
three young dolphins have
found a new game of
chasing their unbroken circle of
snouts and tail fins, while
taking a break from
fishing for their mackerel.

Above, a passing guard of
pelicans remind them to go home.

A last surfer of the day is
sporadically splashed from his board by
yet one more small defiant wave while
the day's baked sand still
feels warm beneath our
just put on sandals that
will walk us along our
long stretch of shallow shoreline
to our long overdue
metered car.

Salt mist is fading to sleep
on the cool horizon.

Such has been
our three days in the sun.

IF I COULD ONLY ASK

This morning, I looked in the mirror, then
looked again, more closely and realized...
I am growing into oldness, and I
sat down and began feeling, for the
first time, some of the understanding
life has tried to teach me. But tomorrow,
when I sit on the park bench with my face
in the streams of the afternoon
the children will ask me things
I still do not know. They will

say to me
why is it that a ladybug is
still able to smile when it is lost?
Or
why does a fallen branch try to stay
close to its mother after
it has been abandoned? They will

say to me
where does a single sock go
after it finally escapes from the dryer?
Or
when does a mountain stream
decide to stop flowing? They will

say to me
how is it possible that a
distant star in the heavens can be
bought and sold to someone's name?

And
what will become of me if the
day comes I forget how to
tie my shoelaces?
Who would even care?

Is it ever too late to know these things?
Is it ever too late to ask?
When our children's children
grow into oldness will we look down
and see them on some park bench with
their faces in the streams of the
afternoon saying,
"If I could only ask…"

WHEN THE WIND
AND THE GRASS
COME TO THE CEDARS

By the time the first breezes would begin sifting
Through the surrounding forest of tall green trees
Her first morning chores were pretty much done.
Lots to do. Always, more to do.
She hated this life. The life she now knew.

This last winter had been real hard on her.
Hard on her and hard on all the other things
she was trying to keep alive.
It had been unusually cold. Not a whole lot of snow.
Just more cold than she could remember.
These first days of spring always
brought the warm winds.
Winds that would blow in the new grass
to reblanket and bring back
new life to her piece of
thawing ground that crept to the edges
of the giant cedar trees.

She was doing the best she knew how.
Struggling.
Surviving.
It was late fall that she had been left alone.

One morning, early, Joe came back in and sat on the
end of their bed complaining of dizziness.
Couldn't get his equilibrium. He was stumbling.

She took his clothes off and laid him back to bed.
The next instant his last breath left him.
He was dead.

She buried him next to the tall cedars.
Fifty-seven years with him. Now she was alone.
Keeping up the things she mostly never had to do.
All the things Joe had solely tended to. But now…

Bending down, she lifted a young piece of grass
from the plotted turf.
Joe's grave wasn't deep enough, she thought.
The wooden cross needed retying. Some new wood.
Later. It would have to wait till later.
In the distance the screech of a
young hawk made her look up.
The pointed tops of the cedars
swayed ever so gently.
By midday the breezes would turn to
stronger, steady winds.
Her eyes turned back
to her husband's grave
as her feet gave way to her knees.

"Damn it, Joe. Damn you, Joe,"
she angrily whispered to herself
in hopeless frustration
pounding her husband's grave with her fist.
"How could you leave me like this?!
It's just not…it…damn you, Joe. Damn…"

She saw where her fist had
smashed down a few
tiny, fresh blades of grass
still in their light green infancy.
She wiped her soiled hand on her stained dress
and coaxed her dried, arthritic fingertips to
fluff up and smooth the new shoots.

She stood and began walking back
toward the barn for some more seed.
Seed left over from last year.
Joe had always done the planting…but…

She hated this life.
This life she now had to bear.
Abandoned.
Scared.
She yearned for the comfort of nightfall.
Tomorrow will be better, she thought.
A little better.

In the high distance
she heard it again.
The faint screech
of the young hawk.
It was its time to soar.
It was the time
when the wind and the grass
come to the cedars.

THE WILLOW

I don't think it is at all
strange, or different. After all,

it was certainly here
before me...the tall willow
with its long, arching
fingers flowing downward.
Softly stroking
always softly stroking
gently swaying to the
day's yielding breeze. So if

you ask me I will tell you
straight out it is not silly at all
to hug a willow tree. There is

a small, flattened
marble stone
that marks my father's grave.
It is among a fetch of stones
just like it in that churchyard.
But there is only one
willow tree there. And it

stands right over his grave
and yes, I can only hope
to suppose it will
be there long after
I am gone as well.

I love to hug that old willow.

This one is for you, dad.

THE OAK AND THE OWL

We all
at times need to sit under a tree.
Some of us have a favorite tree.
Mine was an old squatted oak that stood alone
in a fenced-in cow pasture. It sprouted

gnarled branches and split tangled elbows that
were far from handsome but always set it's
best table of shade for me. It was,

at that time in my life, my best friend
that oak.
I loved to sit under its strong arms and use
what was left of an after school afternoon
to count clovers while
hoping to find some old forgotten words to
not so ancient melodies. And then

I would count the leaves in the tree until
my pupils could no longer separate the
leaves from the sky, sometimes
stubbornly staying indistinct until
the sun slipped behind the wheat.
It was then he would silently glide in and
land just above me. In whispers

of quiet conversation I would tell my stories to
the owl
the two of us cloaked in the early darkness.
My stories of ambitions and dreams he had already
heard and then it was merely a question of
who would start laughing first
when his patience ran thin. They are

all long gone

that old tree and
the cows that grazed near it and
the owl that lived in it but I will
always remember when the owl
would patiently listen and then tell me
to go after and never fear
those wonderful dreams that lie
within the walls of my fragile soul.

THE BOOKSTORE

The wind was getting stronger.
Colder.
It was beginning to rain, hard. So I

ducked from the wet parking lot into
of all places
a bookstore.
One of those bookstores that
everyone has
heard of
been in
big enough to
have its own zip code. Other than

keeping dry there was
nothing much in the
way of interest for me.
Just books
people
lots of em
standing
sitting
laying in the aisles
reading
glancing. I saw

no one in the cooking section.
Odd
that this back of the store corner
should be abandoned but it
offered the perfect refuge. And so

I refuged there amongst
the plethora of cookbooks.
I plucked
something, anything

off the shelf and initiated
my own rendition of the art of
glancing. Well now
what have we here?

A cookbook written by a
former Oakland Raiders pro football coach.
Odd.
But the more I glanced over this
pigskin director's hardcover manuscript
the more I began to
immerse myself in his
recipes, and pictures, and notions…oh my

I hadn't thought I was hungry but
my mouth was watering.
This is good.
I love this recipe book
by this football guy.
Who would ever have known?
Well, now I did.
I gotta have this book.
I have no money.
No credit card.
I just farted.

I have got to get out of here.

I think I would like to
come back here again sometime.

But not right now
not anytime soon.

Where's the door?
Is it still raining outside?

WORM

Have you ever tried explaining
to a worm why it needs to be
placed on the end of a hook
to catch a fish…

neither have I
that is how it is
I dig worms
I have fish to catch and
if you were to ask me
how many fish are left, well
I cannot tell you and
if you were to ask me
how many worms are left
in my garden, well
I can tell you

one

looking straight at me
perched atop a mounded plop of dirt
on my trowel and if it could talk

it might perhaps be asking me
what will I use to
catch fish when the last worm
(which would be this shiny brown Lumbricina)
is gone, well
I cannot tell you

because I had never really
given it much thought till now and
if this tiny worm were to elaborate

it might perhaps tell me how
my garden needs worms to
keep it beautiful and
I should possibly start using
lures instead, which

leads me to believe that perhaps
worms are pretty smart and
just lucky for me that
I heard it from the worm.

YOSEMITE

I have gathered the fallen pine needles
and set them beneath me.
They are cool
almost cold to my backbone
but I am warm
beneath my blanket and the

night universe that parades its stars
like a field of white pulsating diamonds
strewn on a boundless purple carpet.
There is strength in stars. A subtle,
healing sort of power that
bestows a universal harmony. They have

pledged their resolve and I am
feeling at peace with them,
here where I rest with the earth.
I give them sanction to
levitate my consciousness from me and
disentangle it from the pandemonium
that followed me here. Today

I watched waterfalls. I never knew
white water could polish granite walls
with such splendor and authority,
churning, tumbling all day and
through the night, cascading
in distant hypnotic rhythm to
rejoin spirit and body
to the earth. Tonight

for me, and all other creatures here,
they will be our loyal sentinels in this
valley called Yosemite. Tomorrow

my eyes will open to first light,
my nose to forest pine.
My small fire will
warm my hands and
cook my coffee. Perhaps

I shall hike to Glacier Point and leave the valley floor far below.
Or perhaps to the very top of Vernal Falls where
the upper Merced waits for me.
I have witnessed the
wondrous sight of Mirror Lake
in all its reflective sanctuary and
opened my arms to the embrace of
Half Dome's majestic
granite chest. This morning

I had the privilege of
walking in solitude in the
intermittent mist and rain.
I offered a silent prayer at the base of El Capitan, the valley's
foremost giant cathedral.
And I stopped and sat and cried
where only the memories of
the first giant trees remain.

I am here
where I am meant to be.

I am here in this
valley called Yosemite.

THE FOX AND THE SQUIRREL

When you went to the hedge next to where
the creek flows to pick the last
cluster of blackberries this afternoon
did it bother you to think
you were robbing tomorrow's breakfast
from the thrush and her babies?
You need not worry about her. She will

be quite content foraging her
caterpillars and grubs while the
nearby raccoons and skunks
gather their share of
beetles and seeds and such.
They will be busy.
Perhaps too busy to notice
the gray fox hunching in the short weeds
spying the unsuspecting squirrel. But the

the squirrel already sees the twitching
of the fox's tail and quickly
slithers into the thick berry hedge
for protection. The fox

thinks back to her den
where her kits are
hungry and waiting,
and is determined
not to lose her prey as she
stealthily dashes into the hedge.
On the other side, the squirrel
darts into the open at full speed with
the fox close behind. It all

happens so fast, the both of them
zigging and zagging like mirrored
spurts of lightening when suddenly

the fox's hind legs
spin out from under her
giving the squirrel the
one, blink of its eye it needs
to leap onto the tall, slender trunk of a
small, lone pear tree and
climb to safety just beyond
the reach of the fox. It is
now late in the afternoon and
for the fox,
warm blooded food will be
harder to come by.
So, she will collect her kits and
take them to where she remembers
seeing some scatterings of
nuts and grasshoppers. For now

this hunt is over
and the pear tree is where
the fox and the squirrel
say goodnight to each other.

WAY OF THE DREAMCATCHER

On this night, in the pitch-black darkness
in his Ojibway lodge, the child prayed,
"In what way will I dream this night, Grandfather?"
he asked, from his sleeping place where he laid.

Grandfather's spirit softly spoke to him,
"Tonight, when all dreams fill the air
I will make it so that only good dreams and
those that are meant to be come to you there."

Able to see nothing, even with his eyes wide open,
the child listened, laying still.
The wisdom of Grandfather was comforting and
reassuring to him he so faithfully accepted at will.

"I will send to you, child, the spirit of the spider
so that she may weave for you her web and capture
all of the dreams that may drift down upon you
catching them in her pure, woven dreamcatcher."

And so the spider weaves.
With only pure intentions, her web is meant
to catch and hold those dreams tonight that are bad
leaving only the good dreams to fall through that are sent.

The child sleeps.

And so the spider weaves.
And so the spider weaves.

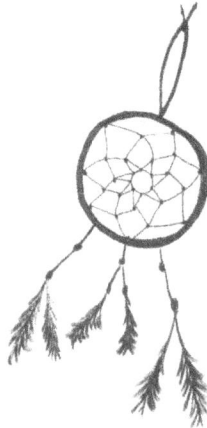

SERENITY

I do not know why
a mockingbird sings
her most beautiful songs
morning after morning
even on those that seem
the most somber of days.

There seems to be such
sweet purpose in her singing.

Can you imagine

having all that joy
bursting at the seams with faith
proclaiming such wonderful
expectancy to the world,
and for the moment
unafraid who is listening?

You have heard her as well and
like you
I try to listen to what she is
singing about, but my ears are
so filled of her enchanting melodies
I do not hear her words.
Perhaps she is not singing in words.
Do you think she is singing in shapes like
the bright stars or
the warm sun or
the trees and flowers…wind?

Keep singing, little songbird.
I will keep listening
and for now
will be quite content to call your songs
my serenity.

THE FROG THAT HELD THE STARS

Oh how she loves escaping to here.
Her sanctuary.
And to know what only
she alone knows is here.

She squints to look.
At first, as the evening sheds its dusk,
it is hard to see. But soon she
finds it where it always is. Over there

just at the feet of the reeds sitting
barely on top of a small piece of
mossed wood is her little
ripple-skinned frog
waiting for her. In its

motionless existence her
tiny companion, every night, speaks solo
love songs to her. Even through its
expressionless dimpled stare
she understands clearly
what her frog sings to her. Oh no

she'll not ever expect to hear so much as
an audible ri-bbit, or, a croak.
Would it be necessary? No, not at all.
And yet, she knows. Every night

she sees her preternaturally
cloaked amphibian surrounded by
millions of quartz white stars
glowing, quivering
in the reflecting mirror of her
tranquil pocket-size lake. She hadn't

been there that long, in the
convalescent home they put her in.
It didn't take her long, though,
to soon find the unlocked
back fence gate that faithfully
rescued her to her very own secret place
where her redeemer sings to her every night.
Her prince.
The frog that held the stars.

Tomorrow's Rose

He held the flower ever so
gently,
delicately,
a small rose richly vibrant,
deep red in color.

He had picked the very last one from
their garden
the last one that still had its
silky soft petals mostly closed.

The tiny crystal misted water droplets had
evaporated from the rose by the time he
brought it to his wife.
Had he surprised her with it? Perhaps.
But somehow, he thought, she knew,
as he had done so
so often before this.

Roses were her favorite.
Especially small red ones.
The thought of this made him glow.
It deepened his love for her
each time, all that much more.

He placed the flower ever so
gently,
delicately
onto his wife's gravestone
with a promise
to bring her another rose
tomorrow.

A FEW SHORT THOUGHTS

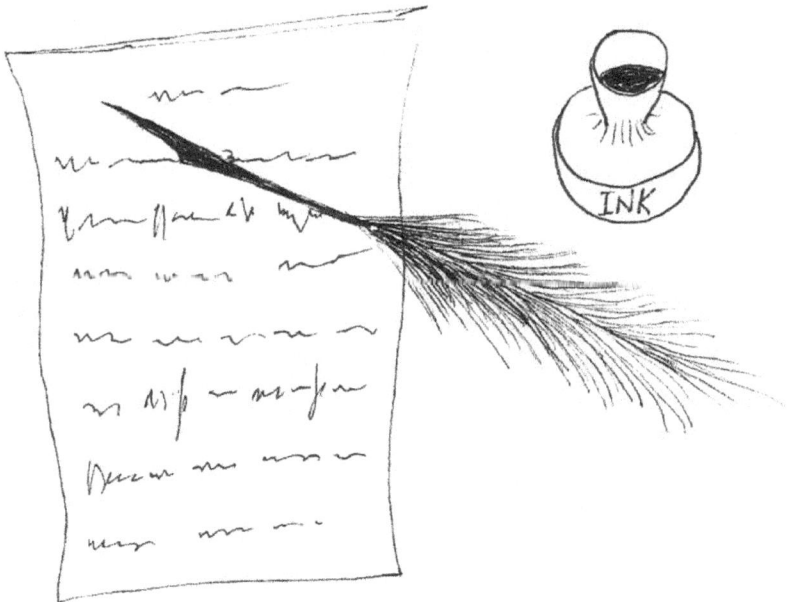

OLD SOFT HANDS

Eternally
    through the
        loving silence
           of old, soft hands
Torn roses from
    our grandchildren's children
        are mended

MOMENTS ON A MANTLE

Extended Pasts
    present windows
        continuous consciousness
          a timely thought
moments found on a soft warm mantle

CHARIOTS OF GOLD

The
child sleeps
in a tranquil void of
glowing, serene
    white light
where yarns of
    astral rays
    spin
        chariots of gold

THE WEAVER

While
the weaver
patiently sewed his
        cloaks of gold
the shadows from his
        dancing candles
laughed and chirped
well into the
        morrow's light

UNHEARD WORDS

Our
unheard words
found configurations of
        hesitations and reservations
shaping motions
        and emotions
within rhythms of
        soft, unbalanced woven plaits

        what I am trying to say is...
                I'm sorry

SUMMER SHOWERS

The early, soft wind laughs when

hot dry mornings
        secretly sing of

dark afternoon
        summer showers

SONGS OF NATURE

Softly rushing waters
        I hear soft rippling in
                velvet gliding songs
singing to ageless rainbows
        throughout warm, rolling winds

LIGHT DREAMS

So lightly I skim…

oft soft winds
  winging their way
    on

heavenly waves
  dancing, prancing
    riding forth
    and

turning moonlit desires

POLITICS

In the very sense of
    buried illusions

vacant peripheral eyes
neither need nor want
    redemption

found in wax-coated views

COMPANIONSHIP

In yet another creation of companionship
a tiny, isolated sphere of light is found
      glittering,
      dancing,
          in the eternal confluent darkness
              space
                    our inner souls

HER SOFT LOCKET

A mother's missed words
      in the end
giving in to echoing memories
      overflowing
      in silent whispers
          from her soft locket

PATIENTLY WAITING

Beyond the playful lights of the
      moon and the
          planets and the
              tingling stars
heaven patiently waits
      tonight
          in calm
          silent
          distant
              peace

ABOUT THE AUTHOR

I write,

in hope of sharing
my poetry and a few thoughts,
hopefully provoking yours.

And if
my writing should perhaps reach inside you
if even just a little
and stir the slightest glimmer,
or
one secluded memory
then

we may say to each other we have met and
it was good and
I thank you, friend.

Lare Joseph Austin

www.ingramcontent.com/pod-product-compliance
Lightning Source LLC
Chambersburg PA
CBHW031339040426
42443CB00006B/394